HAPPY HOUR POETRY

Copyright 2024 by Nikki Van Ekeren.

All rights reserved.

No part of this book may be used or reproduced in any manner whatsoever without written permission from the author, except for the use of brief quotations in a book review.

Your support of the author's rights is appreciated.

Illustrations by Nikki Van Ekeren.

Book Design by Matt Van Ekeren.

Imprint: Independently published.

For information regarding permission or distribution, contact nikkivanekeren@gmail.com

To discover more about the author visit nikkivanekeren.com

ISBN: 978-1-7355066-4-7

when you love
who you are,
every moment
is happy hour

chapter 1
making every hour happy

1. making every hour happy　　　　　　　10
2. poetry martini　　　　　　　　　　　11
3. boho vibes　　　　　　　　　　　　　12
4. gatsby　　　　　　　　　　　　　　　14
5. your best　　　　　　　　　　　　　17
6. shaken or stirred　　　　　　　　　18
7. more cheeky　　　　　　　　　　　　19
8. the journey is never over　　　　　20
9. hollywood glamor　　　　　　　　　22
10. cheers　　　　　　　　　　　　　　24
11. the small things　　　　　　　　　25
12. the willingness　　　　　　　　　　27
13. a day at the museum　　　　　　　28
14. but make it stylish　　　　　　　　30

chapter 2
frank and dean

1. frank and dean　　　　　　　　　　　34
2. take that leap　　　　　　　　　　　36
3. you know the vibe　　　　　　　　　37
4. take a vow to be kind to yourself　　39
5. be the leader that you need　　　　40
6. wherever you go, be there　　　　　41
7. to contribute　　　　　　　　　　　42
8. eat some french fries　　　　　　　45
9. to focus　　　　　　　　　　　　　　46
10. create the character you want to be　48

11. glamor is how you carry yourself	49
12. be brave enough to enjoy	51
13. amor fati	52
14. just for fun	54
15. joie de vivre	56

chapter 3
how you treat yourself

1. how you treat yourself	60
2. decisive ordering	61
3. to toast	63
4. forgiveness	64
5. stretch out into your dream life	65
6. the good is coming your way	66
7. learning is different now	68
8. grace kelly	69
9. your story	71
10. daydream	72
11. work backwards	74
12. decide who to be and go be it	75
13. palm springs	76

chapter 4
dare to live the life you want

1. dare to live the life you want	80
2. the poetry of it all	81
3. curiosity	83
4. the ease of it all	84

5. out in the wild	85
6. be up for it	86
7. champagne	89
8. today	90
9. to the good times	91
10. be here	93
11. let's dance	94
12. discipline	95
13. have that style	97

chapter 5
you are poetry

1. you are poetry	100
2. rembrandt or rothko	102
3. the ability	103
4. be that person	105
5. think happy thoughts	106
6. be a friend to yourself	107
7. live it out	108
8. breakfast at tiffany's	111
9. evoke	112
10. to travel	113
11. reach out to your people	114

chapter 6
truth

1. truth	118
2. today's poetry	119
3. old fashioned	121

4. sculpting the brain	122
5. travel to see yourself	123
6. dapper days	125
7. your ability to decide	126
8. the art of being french	127
9. be in it	128
10. elegance	130
11. when the sculpture reveals itself	131
12. let life come to you	133
13. break down to build back up	134

chapter 7
new people

1. new people	138
2. the culture	140
3. your life is up to you	141
4. practice	143
5. your reality	144
6. let your genius out	145
7. stylize your life	146
8. enjoy it all	148
9. wine and cheese	151
10. last call	152
11. be the poetry	155
12. to simplify	156
13. heading west	158

happy hour poetry

chapter one

making every hour happy

01

making every hour happy

when you share
the fullest version
of who you are
with the world,
it's always happy hour.

when you enjoy
your own company,
you continually
feel inspired by life.

time spent alone
or with others
infuses your eagerness
to be present
and see the poetry all around you.

when you love who you are,
every moment is happy hour.

02

poetry martini

the poem
and the martini.
seemingly simple,
yet impactful and profound.

a group of sentences
you can feel
when you read them.

a sip
you can celebrate
when you drink it.

a grouping
of words
or spirits
that move you so deeply
that your entire life seems to shift
in a moment
to a more powerful place.

03

boho vibes

to embody the bohemian mindset
is to infuse your life
with intention, heart and sentiment.
you have the ability to go with the flow
with purpose and clarity.
you seamlessly connect
with those around you
while never losing your sense of self.

those boho vibes
that effortlessly emanate from your soul
guide you to your purpose.

things seem to come easy to you,
but you know how hard you've worked
to seize such opportunities.
you feel elevated
just by showing up
and being you.
you trust life
and understand the art of patience.

happy hour poetry

04

gatsby

the allure of a story,
the mindset of an era,
and the decadence of pleasure.

the power of the name,
gatsby,
sets the stage for
an endless appetite.

the roaring 20's,
those parties that lasted all night,
the sparkling flapper dresses
and the art deco motifs
set the stage for a timeless story
about a fascinating person
who lived in the moment
and created his own narrative.

embody and exude
the high notes of gatsby.

happy hour poetry

savor those first few sips of champagne
a bit longer,
wear your most stylish outfit
and be in the moment.

van ekeren

05

your best

something changes inside
when you choose
to do your best
at everything you do.

the way you make your morning coffee,
the way you reach out to others,
the way you get dressed
and the way you love your family
are all equal opportunities
to do your best.

when you give your heart
to your life,
your life gives this love back.

you begin to truly embody
your best
and you know
that your best
is always good enough.

06

shaken or stirred

crafting a cocktail
is a lot like
constructing the inner narrative
of your life.

the ingredients
wait for your experimentation
and direction.

take
one part of this
and another part of that
and shake it all up
(or stir it).

then add a little something extra
and serve it up.

be bold in your stemware
as in your style of living.

celebrate the creation you've crafted
and bask in your uniqueness.

07

more cheeky

today,
be a little more cheeky.
have a little more fun.
take things in with a broader perspective.

laugh a bit more,
lean into your beautiful life
and be light hearted.
be bold in how you share
your style and energy.

you will find
that this seemingly light spirit
carries more strength with it
than you can imagine.

08

the journey is never over

your journey is never over
while you still have breath in your lungs.
you will never stop growing,
becoming
and evolving.
enjoy this truth.
savor the pains of change
and bask in the calmness of surrender.
you can only control your effort
and your attitude.
the world may or may not reward you.
accept it all
and make poetry out of it.

happy hour poetry

09

hollywood glamor

the level of elegance
and glamor
that you bring to the room
lies in your mindset,
not in your status,
wealth
or career.
remember this.
embody that hollywood glamor
that just oozes its own brand of confidence.
be audacious for no reason.
seek to enjoy
rather than to impress.

happy hour poetry

van ekeren

10

cheers

by commemorating
an occasion,
a feeling
or a moment,
you elevate it.
by declaring a moment special,
you heighten
its impact,
memory
and aura.
say
"cheers"
more often.
celebrate the mundane
to make it
magical.

11

the small things

the small things
connect the dots
and weave together
a large and beautiful life.
the way you feel after you smile for no reason,
the way that first sip of coffee tastes,
the way the air smells at night,
or even the way a good book
can make you feel,
it is all those little things
that create the foundation
for pure happiness.

van ekeren

12

the willingness

be steadfast in your willingness
to grow in your journey.
lean into the discomfort
this willingness may evoke.
face the things you need to.
do the work.
be willing to thrive and let go
of the victim mindset.
this willingness
can become your new norm.
invite life in.
let it sculpt you.

13

a day at the museum

when you choose
to go to the museum,
your intention
elevates the way you see.
you have decided to be in the midst
of greatness,
aspiration
and innovation.
a museum encourages you
to enhance your perspective.
you begin to see a through line
throughout all of humanity.
a desire to discover,
to improve
and then to share such findings.
art is a framed moment in alchemy.

happy hour poetry

14

but make it stylish

anything
can be stylish.
the way you walk to the train station,
the way you wash the dishes,
the way you put on your shoes
or even the way you eat a meal.

have fun with your life.
enjoy the work that comes along
with being human.
you get to nurture and care
for yourself.
honor this role.

do you,
but make it stylish.

happy hour poetry

van ekeren

happy hour poetry

chapter two

frank and dean

01
frank and dean

dean martin
and frank sinatra
evoke the aura of a nostalgic time.
an era when suits were worn by most,
martinis were ordered in pairs
and lounge acts headlined in las vegas.
a time when the rat pack
drank and joked on stage
while the audience drank and laughed along
with them.
frank and dean
convey the essence of this era
and an artful
yet laid back approach to living.

happy hour poetry

van ekeren

02

take that leap

you know where you want to go
and who you want to be.

accept the fact
that this journey will take
inner and outer work.

face any fears
that surround
this elevated version of you.
this fear
may be rooted
in a haze
of unworthiness.

let this go.
take that leap
and become the person that you want to be.
just decide to be worthy of it all
and you
magically
will be.

03

you know the vibe

it is that feeling,
knowing
you will always love yourself.
it is being okay with yourself
when you mess up.
it is knowing that you will never be perfect.

you know the vibe
and how to create it
from within.
it is self love
and it's always
one thought away.

van ekeren

04

take a vow to be kind to yourself

as of today,
at this moment,
take the vow
to be kind to yourself.

this intention will feed your soul.
this knowing will guide you
to your best life.
if something is not right for you,
do not do it.

remember exactly
who you are,
love yourself
and seek inner nourishment.

05

be the leader that you need

lead

your life.

feel the energy in the room

and own it.

know who you are

and where you are going.

lead.

shape.

mold.

sculpt your life

into the one you want.

06

wherever you go, be there

let go of the desire
to be everything to everyone
and be everywhere.
let go of the need for attention.

wherever you go,
be there.

open up your eyes
to the beauty that's all around you
and within you.
celebrate this moment.
celebrate your truth.
let this be your fuel
rather than the approval and attention
from others.

be present.
be there.
enjoy it all.

07

to contribute

instead of being an expert,
be a contributor.
share.
collaborate.
be present.
stand up tall.
be happy.

see the world around you.
see yourself.
be.

be the person who helps out,
who shares what they know in real time,
who is generous,
optimistic
and most importantly,
happy.

happy hour poetry

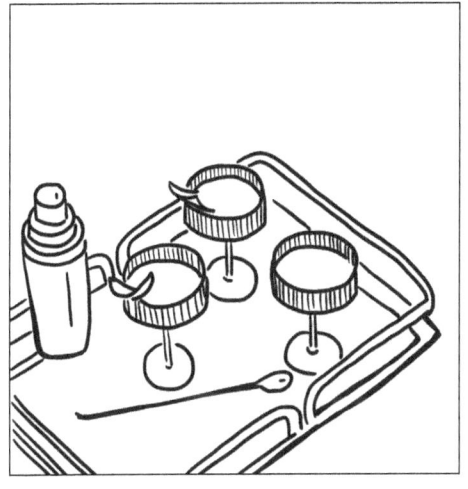

van ekeren

08

eat some french fries

there are times for improving
and then there are times for indulging.
a life well lived
understands
the dichotomy of it all.
it sounds hypocritical
yet
it is not.
it is nuanced.
life is full of nuances
and small differences
that seem large.
go live your life
out loud.
be bold about changing your mind.
just have fun with it all
and eat some french fries.

09

to focus

allow your goals
to inform your focus.
what you spend your time on
will grow.
reach for what matters.
clarify what you want your life to be.
define who you want to be.
focus on getting there
and you will.

happy hour poetry

10

create the character you want to be

your life

is your ultimate work of art.

create the character

that you want to be

and go be it.

enjoy your own company.

smile at your attempts

and congratulate yourself

on whatever outcomes present themselves.

you get to be you.

you have the honor of sculpting

your unique character

and inhabiting that space.

11
glamor is how you carry yourself

there is no need to rush
anything in life.
you have this one moment
that you are living.
so be in it
fully.
embody a light hearted
and graceful approach to life.
feel it.
embody it.
experience it.
glamor is how you carry yourself,
so choose it.
it'll guide you,
nourish you
and create your dream life.

van ekeren

12

be brave enough to enjoy

bravery
is being
happy in the moment you are in.
it is showing up
with a smile on your face.
the act of enjoying
feels vulnerable,
yet it is actually so powerful and strong.

be brave enough to enjoy
your life.
share your essence
with those around you.
let the world
know that you embody joy.

amor fati

the greatest gift
you can give yourself
is to learn
to love
whatever life delivers to you.

amor fati
as the stoics called it.

a
love
of
fate.

when you begin to accept life
and create the narrative around it,
you become the sculptor.

you become
as you are becoming.

happy hour poetry

14

just for fun

climb into the mindset
that encourages you
to do things
just for fun.
feel this state of being.
embody this infectious energy
and share it with others.
the art of having fun
should be cultivated
and celebrated.

happy hour poetry

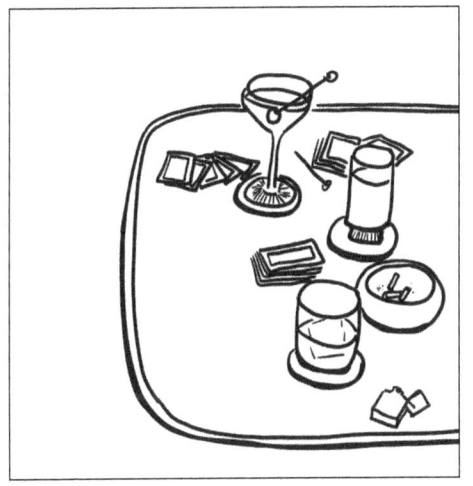

15

joie de vivre

to embody
joie de vivre
is to enjoy life
through all of your senses
and to share this joy.

this approach to life
lies in the ability to
access your most authentic self
and live in this pocket of pure confidence.

it is when
you are contagiously joyful,
wildly hopeful
and enjoy the art of living.

happy hour poetry

van ekeren

happy hour poetry

chapter three

how you treat yourself

01

how you treat yourself

you are
the result of
how you
treat yourself.
how you do one thing
is how you do most things.
the little private moments
add up
to become
your entire life.

how do you interact with yourself
in the
in-between times?
if you do not love every second of it,
change it
today.

happy hour poetry

02

decisive ordering

don't you love it
when someone
is decisive
when they order at a restaurant?
why not parlay this tactic
into your daily life
and become
more confident in your decisions.
choose that path.
order that cocktail.
feel how the art of being decisive
fuels your feelings of self independence.

van ekeren

03

to toast

how lovely it is
to toast
to a moment,
to a life well lived,
to an occasion
or to an ordinary night.
you get to narrate
the story of your life.
you get to celebrate
the big and small moments.
toast
to it all
and enjoy every second of it.

04

forgiveness

the easiest path to happiness
is forgiveness.
to forgive others
is to forgive yourself.
this decision sets your soul free
and intentionally guides your life
to its most magical realms.
forgiveness is alchemy in action.
it erases the pain and creates
beauty and joy
in an instant.

05

stretch out into your dream life

stretch out
into your dream life.
discover how near it actually is.
be the person
that lives
this dream life.

as you read those words,
perhaps you felt some anxiety.
the questions of worth,
of value,
of ability
and of logistics
creep in.
this is okay.

your dreams
are reachable.
keep stretching.
do so with grace,
focus
and trust.

van ekeren

06

the good is coming your way

sometimes
the good
is cloaked in pain,
in hardships
and in challenges.
but,
everything is for your good.
know this.
live by this.

happy hour poetry

07

learning is different now

you learn
by doing,
by seeing,
by mirroring,
not by memorizing and proving yourself to others.

you learn
from sensing how
and why.

you learn
by seeking
and discovering
and taking notes
and developing an inner sense of reassurance.

08

grace kelly

her elegance is still felt
when one speaks her name.
the grace
of grace kelly
will continue to inspire those
who seek classic beauty.

her presence is still felt
when you watch one of her movies.
she spoke with fervor
and intent
and always carried herself with style.

grace kelly
is a mood,
a look,
an attitude,
to aspire to
for all time.

van ekeren

09

your story

just remember
that your story
is your art
and it is a brave act
to share it.

your story
is the world expressing itself
through you.

lean into it.
be generous with it.
enjoy sharing it.

10

daydream

let your mind rest
on a happy topic.
stay there.
lean into it.
reach further.
merge with it.
wander into the stories
that make you feel free
and autonomous
and brave.
allow yourself to daydream
as the hero of every story.
you are the person
that you've always wanted to be.
see yourself
within
and around.
wander into your daydreams
with curiosity
and joy.

happy hour poetry

11

work backwards

you already know
the ending,
work backwards from this.
slowly walk yourself back
from the ending of your story
until
now.
what do you want to do,
to see,
to create?
how does it happen?
write the story
and then go live it.

12

decide who to be and go be it

ralph waldo emerson said
"the only person
you are destined to become
is the person you decide to be."

you acquired certain habits and tendencies
during your childhood.
do you want to be those things
or do you want to be something else?

honor your family
by being the best person
that you are willing and capable
of being.
stretch out.
flex new muscles.

do something
that helps you grow
everyday.

13

palm springs

the place
where the desert
meets the sky.
time and space
seem to bend and blur
with muted colors of nature.

the stoic mountains
that surround the city
intertwine with the colorful
modern architecture
while the poetic palm trees
sway in the wind.

the essence of palm springs
sings with the voice
of an old soul.

the city conjures up iconic images
captured on film
by slim aarons
and continues to convey an era
of another time.

happy hour poetry

van ekeren

happy hour poetry

chapter four

dare to live the life you want

01

dare to live the life you want

you know
what you want.
deep down,
you know.
it is something pure
and original
and true.
you know who you are
and who you are becoming.
dare to be
the version of you
that excites you.
merge with this version
of yourself
and share your essence with the world.

02

the poetry of it all

this moment
may feel ordinary,
but it is
poetry in action.
you have created the life you now live,
you have forged connections between others,
you have opened up this book
to read this poem
and you are breathing in fresh air.
the poetry of it all
is so beautiful
and life affirming.
take a moment to be in it.

van ekeren

03

curiosity

get hooked on your own curiosity.
live through the lens of it.

be humbled with the simplicity
of childlike wonder.

life is simple,
yet complex.

your curiosity will always guide you.
be humble
and excited
about it all.

04

the ease of it all

when you feel connected
to your true self,
the world can't sway you.
you are anchored in your truth.
the things that used to trigger you
do not have that same influence.
you are able to go with the flow
and be present.

the ease of it all
makes life feel more poetic.
the small things
connect the dots
and weave together
a large and beautiful life.

05

out in the wild

heading out for happy hour
can signify the end of one part of your day
and the beginning of another.
you could have a drink at home
or you could have one
out in the wild.
it is where
the clattering sounds of a bar
magically comfort part of you.
it is venturing
out into the unknown
where you never know who you will meet.
it is that mixture
of architecture, mood and people.
it is your home
away from home.

06

be up for it

life
is going to give you challenges.
be up for it.
lean into it.
proclaim
"you're exactly what i wanted.
let's do this."
and go about your merry way.

happy hour poetry

van ekeren

07

champagne

isn't it amazing
that the mention
of a certain type of beverage
connotes
a particular feeling and mood.

champagne.
the art of
opening the bottle,
drinking it
and savoring it.

the tone of the word,
the region in where it derived,
the stemware it requires
the elevated sense of occasion it evokes,
all poetic,
fun
and festive.

08

today

everything starts today.
what a gift it is
to be alive
and with the company we keep.

today
is the gift that keeps on giving.

celebrate who you are
and where you are
today.

make the past
as you go.

happy hour poetry

09

to the good times

to the nights
that
we want to last forever.
to the people
who make us feel like ourselves.
to the person
that sees us fully
and helps us become our fullest self.
to the desires
that feel good to fulfill.
to the lives
we keep creating.
to the good times
that we get to be a part of.

van ekeren

10

be here

the world is
continually inviting you
to
be here
now.

anchor yourself
into the present moment.
feel its gentle pull
and surrender to it.
experience
this moment
exactly where you're at.

be here now.

11
let's dance

let's dance.
turn on a jazz album
and let's just listen
and be
and dance.
let's feel the music and one another.
let's discover our rhythm again.
let's pretend that we are at a
cool jazz club
in our finest clothes.
let's get swept away in the music,
in the experience.

12

discipline

discipline
creates
more discipline.

just as
success
creates more success.

you begin to catch your rhythm
and lock into a higher version of yourself.
it feels so good
that you don't want to stop.

so, do the thing
that you've always wanted to do.
be the person that makes you happy.

van ekeren

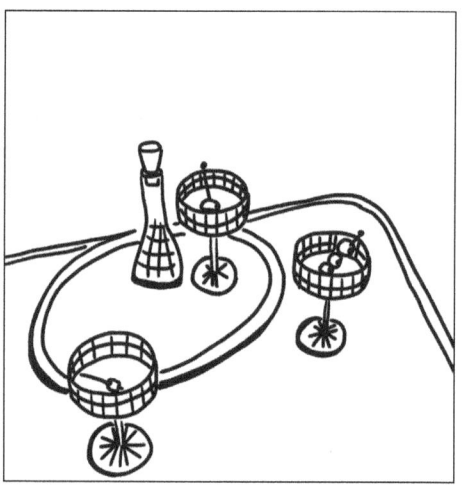

13

have that style

when you have
that style
that loves living,
life opens up doors for you.
it feels good to live.

you are able to celebrate the everyday
and truly enjoy the big or little things.

when you have
that style that jumps into life,
you love people
and their company.

van ekeren

happy hour poetry

chapter five

you are poetry

01

you are poetry

let your life
be the most magical poetry
ever created.

let yourself be happy
and know that this feeling is up to you.

if you want to be happy
think happy thoughts.
that's the only way to get there.

being the poetry
means
deciding what you want
and going after it.

it means choosing yourself.
it means letting go of bad habits
and embracing self discipline.

happy hour poetry

02

rembrandt or rothko

a painting can
translate
a vivid mood
through its presence,
imagery
and aura.
just as the words of a poem
can shift your perspective on life,
a painting can change the way you see.

the way a piece by rembrandt
makes you feel versus
one by rothko.
the realist and the abstract
both extract certain impressions
on you as the viewer.

it's not about choosing what is better,
it is the art of learning how to see
it all
and let the work of another
elevate your sense of being.

03

the ability

the ability to eat, drink, and be merry
is a great gift to behold

it is such an honor to tune into
the art of enjoyment.

the inner muscles needed to enjoy
are few,
yet they need to be flexed
continuously
to stay healthy.

smile from ear to ear.
does this make you feel happy?
smile again.
awh, there's that feeling.

van ekeren

04

be that person

you know that person
who just exudes joy and happiness?
it is that person
who defines
their own narrative.

someone who is
the star of their story.
someone who shares their
energetic essence.

someone who is
decisive and confident
and only needs to be
exactly where they're at.

be that person.

05

think happy thoughts

if you want to be happy,
think happy thoughts.
do the work
you need to do
to keep your mindset elevated.
stop blaming others.
stop feeling guilty.
no emotion is yours.
everything is just passing
through your mindset.
you can be whoever you want to be.
think happy thoughts.
let them wash over your pain,
sorrow,
or shame
and transmute these low feelings
into pure joy.

06

be a friend to yourself

"what progress have I made?"
seneca wrote,
"I am beginning to be my own friend."

extend that hand toward yourself.
love yourself.
be kind to yourself.
be a friend to yourself.
snuggle into your own energy
and enjoy the journey.

07

live it out

you're going to live out
what is within you.

if you don't like what you're living,
change your inner narrative.

elevate your
ability to cast yourself
as the hero
of your story.

live out
your dream life.

happy hour poetry

van ekeren

08

breakfast at tiffany's

sometimes
it's the idea,
the aura of it,
the wonderment of it all
that drives you.

it's that moment
when you let go of fear
and start to reach for your dreams.
you begin to believe
that you can aspire and achieve.

you summon your dreams
into reality.

you'll take
your breakfast
at tiffany's
now.

09

evoke

embody
and evoke the essence within you.
allow the spirit within
to merge
with those around you.
the connection to the spirits one drinks
and the spirit within
is a fascinating metaphor.
evoke the spirit
that elevates your entire being.

10

to travel

traveling
is equal parts
inspiring and humbling.

it sharpens your grace and grit
and elevates your mind.

enjoy it all.
lean into the
awkward and uncomfortable
moments.
forgive yourself for not knowing it all.

to travel
is to become.
bask in the journey.

11

reach out to your people

the art of correspondence
is a true gift.
learn it
and practice it
and you will live a fulfilled life.
it feels good
to connect with friends and family.
it is special to have people
who care about you.
reach out to your people
and let them know that you care.

happy hour poetry

van ekeren

happy hour poetry

chapter six

truth

01

truth

be clear
in your truth.
allow the light to shine
on all parts of you.
you are in your truth now.
hear it.
feel it.
listen to it.
discover more of it.

02

today's poetry

when yesterday's moments
become
today's poetry.

when the banal
becomes the beautiful
because you deemed it so.

when you learn how to create
the inner feelings
that reflect the outer life you crave.

life becomes poetry
when you are fully present in it
and carefully shape the narrative of it all.

van ekeren

happy hour poetry

03

old fashioned

when you order
an old fashioned
at the bar,
you seem to settle into a new time,
a different era,
a more dapper day.
you are completely aware
of your presence at the bar
and the work ahead
for the bartender.
when you order
an old fashioned,
you know that you are moments away
from the most exciting drink of your day.

04

sculpting the brain

reading
is for
sculpting
the mind.

you get to choose
what you put into your brain
and then experience
its essence.

cunningly curate
the contents
of your mind.

05

travel to see yourself

when you travel,
your eyes begin to see new things.
the people who live in the new city you are
visiting
appear alluring
and magical.
their confidence seems to project
from their ability to be present.
are you seeing yourself in them?
perhaps,
you travel
to see yourself
with new eyes.

van ekeren

happy hour poetry

06

dapper days

your dapper days
are always within you.
your best style
is a constant companion.
stay curious about the world,
the culture,
the fashion of the day
and maintain your staple pieces.

dress up
to go the store.
wear your most expensive bag
on a walk around the park this afternoon.
put on your favorite necklaces,
bracelets and rings
while you watch tv at home in your pajamas.

your dapper days
are happening now
and will never come to an end.

07

your ability to decide

once you flex the muscle of decision making,
you will be in awe of its power.
explore your ability to decide
who you want to be
and how you want to act.
this could be a new career choice
or how you present yourself to the world
or even how you order your favorite drink.

happy hour poetry

08

the art of being french

the french allure,
their way of living
and disposition
revolve around one main habit—
discipline.
at first glance,
the french appear so chic and calm,
yet they are that way
from years of preparation and work.
from an early age,
the french focus
on their inner and external values.
they put these life characteristics
at the forefront of their efforts.
those chic
seemingly thrown together looks
are the result of research,
work and effort.
the art of being french
relies on the beautiful lifelong habit
of discipline.

09

be in it

your life is happening now,
be in it.
celebrate
and enjoy it.

allow
the poetic pull
of nostalgia
to shape the current moment.

curate today's memories
by fully surrendering to it.

happy hour poetry

10

elegance

the tone of elegance
can be felt
at any moment in your life.
the only prerequisite to experience elegance
is a confidence in oneself
and one's abilities.
you can be elegant
while drinking your tea at home
or walking to the market.
you can exude elegance
in your most dapper attire
or even your most casual.
elegance comes from within
and is cultivated over a lifetime.
do not wait for another
to deem you as "elegant"
know who you are
and what you are capable of bringing
to the world.

11

when the sculpture reveals itself

there is a moment in everyone's life,
when your truth is revealed.
it feels as if the sculpture reveals itself from a
slab of marble.

from the clay,
from the unknown,
from the pain and the sacrifice,
from all of the love you've bestowed,
you begin to see yourself and the life you lead.

you see how easy it is to do the right thing.
you understand what work to do
and devote your life to it.

when the sculpture reveals itself,
when your life opens up to you,
when you are certain of everything you used
to be unsure of,
you feel so grateful to be alive.

van ekeren

12

let life come to you

project love
and receive love.
let life come to you.
announce your presence
by being present
in every room you enter.
create your own luck
by showing up,
being prepared
and seizing opportunities.
let life come to you
by reaching toward it.

13

break down to build back up

the life that you are living
is yours.
make sure
you know this.
stop fearing
what you have been trained to feel.
start creating the new experiences,
new feelings
and the new state of mind
that you truly want.

happy hour poetry

van ekeren

happy hour poetry

chapter seven

new people

01

new people

allow yourself
to chat with a new person
about trivial things.
those small conversations
are actually
very meaningful.
small talk
can feel like
big talk
when you open up to it.
feel the energy of new people.
enjoy the discomfort
of new things.
you will begin to look forward to it
rather than dread it.
life is so big
yet so small.
allow those little conversations
to evoke magic.

happy hour poetry

02

the culture

life generates
new cultural norms
very quickly.
it is not about staying on trend
with the culture,
it is about staying on trend
with yourself.

03

your life is up to you

choose
to behold wonder
rather than to be fearful.
your life
is up to you.
narrate the story
that you want to hear.
envision the beauty
that you want to see.
start curating
the walls within your mind.

van ekeren

04

practice

if you want to feel good,
learn how to create the emotion from within.

deconstruct
what happiness feels like to you
and work at recreating it.
rehearse how amazing this feels.

remember this process
and trust your ability
to summon feeling good.

it is truly
just a thought away.
the more you practice it,
the more happiness you will experience.

05

your reality

your reality
is yours
to create.
if something happens to you,
realize that it is happening for you.

your reality
is elevated when
you no longer fear
your truth.

you understand that
your reality is comprised
of pain and delight.

the people around you
will make up stories to define their reality.
let them.
you know your truth
and have vowed
to create your own sustainable
and nourishing reality.

06

let your genius out

let your genius out
by believing in it.
much has been written
about one's inner genius.

see the genius within
and around.

remember to be in awe
just
because
you're alive
and a part of something bigger than you are.

wander about
for no reason
other than to explore
and report back.
reach for your inner genius
and ignite its power.

07

stylize your life

go ahead,
romanticize your life.
see it in style.
live it in style.

if one
wants to criticize your point of view,
let them.

you get to see
the world
as you want to see it.

happy hour poetry

08

enjoy it all

have the attitude
of jovial acceptance
to it all.
try to believe
in the phrase:
"you're just what
i was looking for"
with everything that happens to you.

own your fate.
love your fate.
work on your reaction
to it all.
let your mind
create the poetry
that you seek in life.

happy hour poetry

van ekeren

happy hour poetry

09

wine and cheese

how lucky one is
to open up a bottle of wine
with another
and chat over
wine and cheese.

the goal of the moment
is to enjoy,
to connect
and to discuss.

there is a celebratory tone
in the air
full of lively conversation
and laughter.

being present
is the present
as the wine, cheese and chatting continue.

10

last call

make it a fun night,
maybe even stay for last call.
enjoy the people you are with
and enjoy your own company.
stretch out energetically.
do not look back,
be in the moment.
stop regretting.
you will never be perfect.
project your energy
rather than ingest anothers.
when in doubt,
be energetically bold.

happy hour poetry

van ekeren

11

be the poetry

see the poetry.
be the poetry.
let your eyes see the beauty
that is always around you.
let yourself be inspired
by the purity
of it all.

beauty is a decision.
beauty is inner kindness.
beauty is a feeling
that is easy to inhabit.

12

to simplify

the best times
in life
usually do not involve much..

to romanticize a life,
simplify it.
remember who you are
and what makes you original.

be creative.
sculpt the life you want.
reach toward your soul
and the souls of those around you.
simplify your life
by finding your center
over and over again.

happy hour poetry

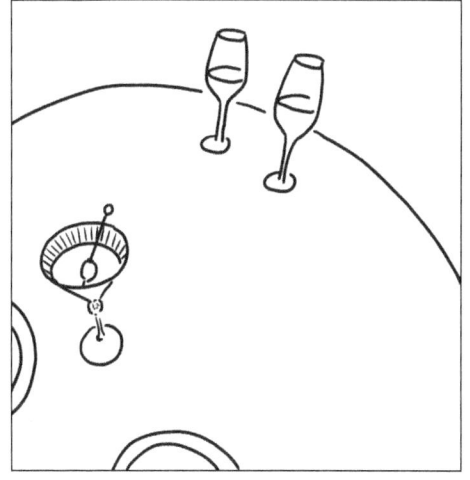

13

heading west

the west
symbolizes a place
where you can dream
and create.

the open spaces
and
the color palette of light and nature
elevate the way
you can see
and be.

it's almost as if this place
creates a
more malleable
frame of mind
to shape your inner world.

the wild west
let's
your inner wild
run free.

happy hour poetry

van ekeren

About the Author

Nikki Van Ekeren is a writer and an artist.

Her work is rooted in optimism, self growth and celebrating oneself.

Nikki's other books include *Poems on Style*, *Grace & Grit*, *These Poems Are About Sunny Days*, *Palm Trees and Possibilities*, and for children, *You Get to Be You*.

www.ingramcontent.com/pod-product-compliance
Lightning Source LLC
Chambersburg PA
CBHW061747070526
44585CB00025B/2826